EX LIBRIS

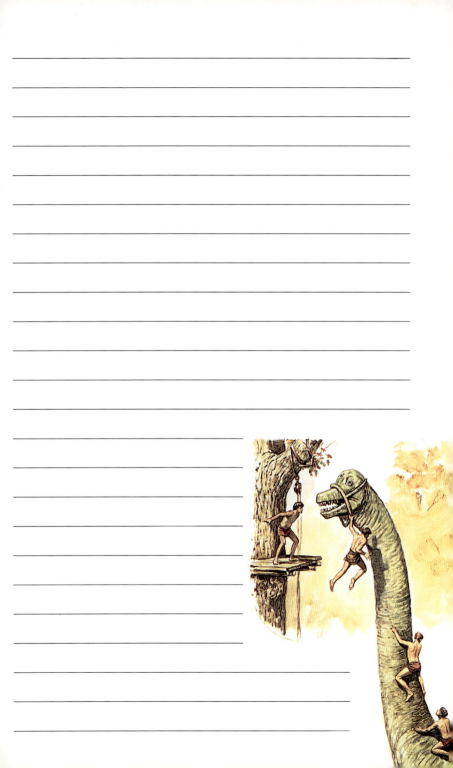

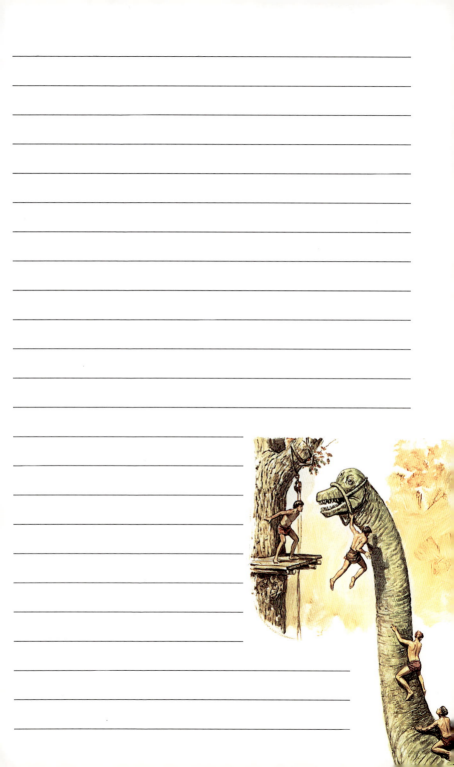

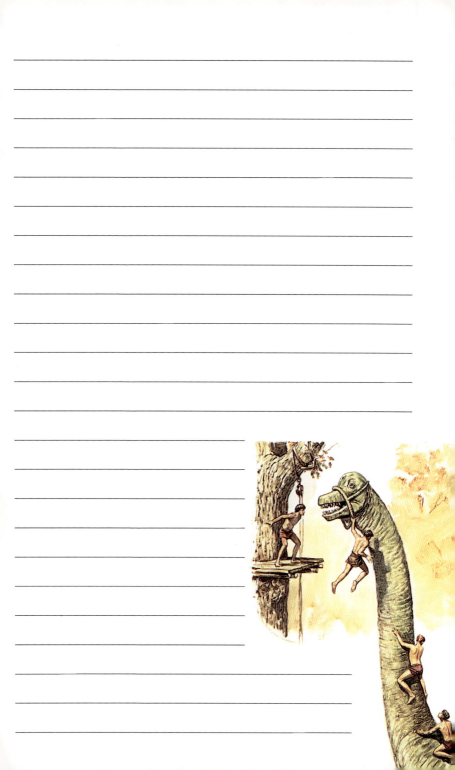

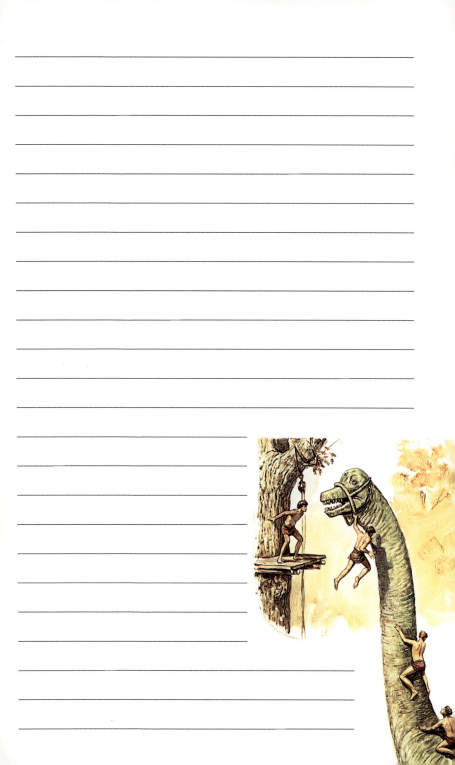

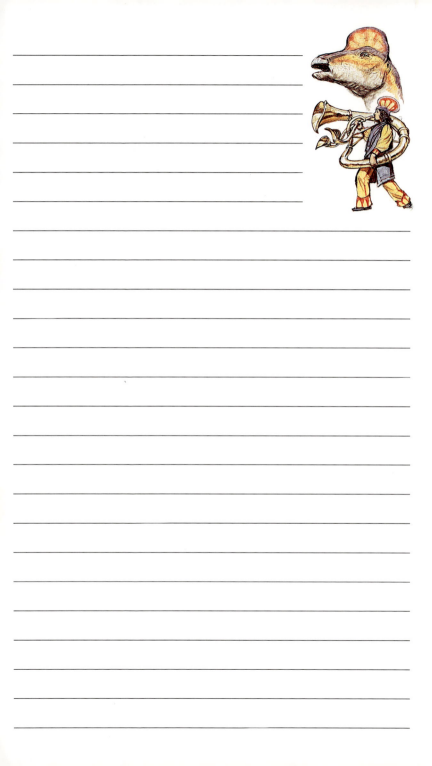

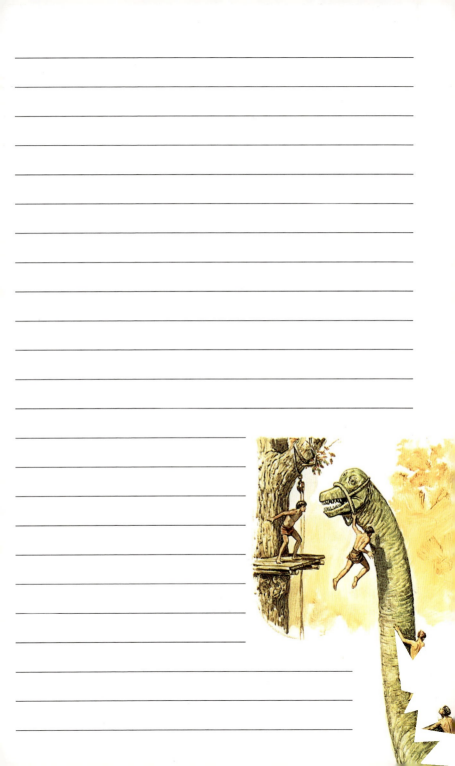

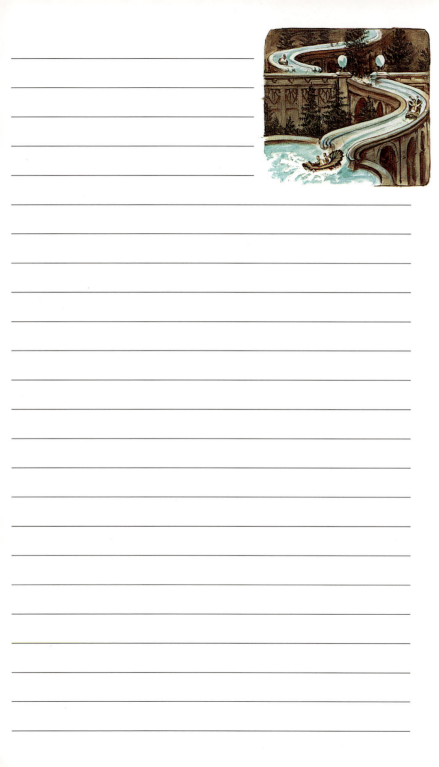

Morning Reflections, © *1990 James Gurney*
The dinosaurs and humans of Dinotopia share a great
appreciation for music. Here a Stegosaurus and a young
man enjoy a musical interlude on the shores of a calm lake.